HEDGEROW
WINE MAKING
Journal

www.AlmostOffGrid.com
Brew, Make, Forage, Grow.

 almostoffgridbev    almostoffgrid    almostoffgrid

Why Almost Off Grid?

Living Off Grid is a term usually associated with people aiming to be self-sufficient with no dependency on the outside world, whilst minimising their impact on the environment. Living this way typically involves making and repairing things using traditional methods which were developed before utility companies existed and modern production methods were invented.

We love the idea of moving our family and business completely off grid, but that would be a huge step for most families in the UK, including us. But living in a way that reduces our dependency on large corporations, minimises our impact on the environment, and revives traditional crafts: we are up for that. As, it seems, are many other people.

Our favourite quote by Arthur Ashe is how we live: "Start where you are. Use what you have. Do what you can.'

So we grow many of our own vegetables in the summer when it's easy to do, using permaculture principles where possible. Otherwise, we buy them. We make most of our own drinks, but not all of them. We are decreasing our carbon footprint each year, through solar panels, an electric car, a heat pump and battery storage technology in our home and business, but we still enjoy the usual modern conveniences. We occasionally make our own clothes, certainly not all the time.

We started using the term 'Almost Off Grid' to describe the way our life has changed over the past 10 years, and it stuck. So when we opened our homebrewing shop, Almost Off Grid was the obvious name for it.

This journal series came about because we realised we had masses of books on all sorts of subjects, but many of them are sitting on the shelf largely unused. When you buy a book on a topic that interests you, such as home brewing, you tend not to use all of it. Some of it appeals or is useful, some doesn't or isn't. Almost Off Grid Journals are designed to be different. They cover a range of subjects related to traditional crafts and sustainable living. Each one has an overview of the subject, room in the margins for notes, and lots of lined pages. You can then add your own information and clippings as you build your knowledge, allowing you to create the perfect reference series just for you.

Other journals in the series include:

Number 1: Mead Making
Number 3: Country Wine Making
Number 4: Cider Making

Contents

About us

I'm Bev Toogood and I run an independent homebrewing and food-making shop with my husband, Andy. Our shop is located in Horam, East Sussex in an area of outstanding natural beauty.

Starting a homebrewing business was an obvious next step for us, as we have brewed our own wine, cider and mead for many years. We are proud to occupy our premises in Horam High Street, just as businesses before us have for over a century.

In the front of this journal, you will find an overview of hedgerow wine making, including a wine maker's foraging calendar, then five tried and tested recipes to get you started. This is followed by over 100 lined journal pages for you to record your hedgerow wine making notes.

We sell everything you need to get started in our shop at AlmostOffGrid.com. I also have a blog there where you will find more wine recipes. On the blog, I give advice on brewing, fermenting, and making your own everything, together with hints and tips for living in a more sustainable way.

Happy Brewing!

Bev

About This Book

Almost Off Grid Living Journal 2: Hedgerow Wine Making

If you've never made wine before, the vast array of books, recipes and winemaking terminology can seem daunting. This journal aims to cut through the jargon and make it simple - for that's really how hobby winemaking should be. It will then go on to be the best hedgerow winemaking book you own, because you created it just for you.

The first homebrew we attempted was cider. Because I'm me, I spent many hours reading all the advice I could find, and every recipe out there. I ended up (unintentionally) choosing a rather more complex one than I needed. Our first attempt at homemade cider was not great, but it didn't put us off.

I say it all the time but this bears repeating. Homebrewing can be as simple, or as complex, as you want to make it. Tried and tested recipes are always the best starting point, rather than finding something random on the internet with no evidence that anyone has ever successfully made it.

The hedgerow wine recipes in this book can be made when the main ingredients are in season. Plus some of the fruits and flowers are available dried, such as elderflowers, so those recipes can be made all year round. They are all suitable for beginners. Rather than give you one 'starter recipe', which may not be possible to make if you can't source the ingredients, this journal contains 5 recipes which are all suitable for beginners. The one you make first is likely to depend on when you stumble upon this journal.

We will go into more depth about foraging for your ingredients a little later.

There is one important thing I need to say at the start, and it cannot be emphasised enough. Please ensure you are 100% certain that you have identified your fruit and flowers correctly before picking them, and certainly before turning them into wine for you or others to consume.

About Hedgerow Wine Making

"Where there is no wine there is no love."
- Euripides

People have been creating fermented drinks from hedgerow ingredients for centuries. They have either done that by design, or by accident when fruits were left in warm conditions and naturally fermented of their own accord. When you turn fruit and/or flowers that you have foraged into wine, you have made a hedgerow wine.

Whilst some homemade wines can still taste a bit rough, much as I want to like them, many humble hedgerow ingredients can be turned into a really nice drink. They cost just about nothing to make and the final wine reminds you of the sunny day when you picked the ingredients.

So what is a hedgerow wine compared with other wines? In the absence of a clear definition, here's mine. Hedgerow wines are made from foraged fruit and flowers, country wines are from cultivated varieties of fruit and vegetables we grow or buy (strawberries, apples, peaches). Traditional wines are made from grapes. However, it is not unusual for these three sets of ingredients to overlap, and sometimes you may use all three.

So, for example, you might use juice from a cultivated apple variety you have growing in your garden. Or you might add grape juice concentrate to a hedgerow wine recipe. There are examples of such recipes in this book. The reason I include them is not to try to sell you grape juice concentrate when you don't need it (I run a homebrew shop remember) but because I have tried these recipes with and without grape juice added. It can make a big difference to the depth and body of homemade wine, and I prefer to add juice rather than chemical additives to achieve the same effect. That said, not all additives are evil by any means. More about those later.

A final word. Sometimes commercial fruit wines have flavourings added after the wine process is finished. This is to make the wine taste more like the fruit named on the label, because that's what the consumer expects to taste. Your homemade wine will taste lovely, but it may not taste as strongly of the fruit or flowers as shop bought ones do because you haven't added flavourings to them.

The Basic Wine Making Process

People typically buy their drinks in supermarkets, rather than make them. Hence we have become used to the taste of commercially produced wines. At some stage, homemade wine became a bit of a poor relation. That is changing. People are starting to return to these old crafts, which is a blessing.

The basic process for making wine hasn't changed very much over time, and is pretty similar whether you're a professional, commercial or hobby winemaker.

But hobby winemaking will produce a different wine from those you buy, not least of all because of the ingredients you're using. So keep in mind that a dandelion wine is never going to taste like a sauvignon blanc. It just isn't. But it can be equally lovely.

With that in mind, the basic steps for making any wine are as follows. If you're thinking 'that's not much doing with rather a lot of waiting', you're right. It is.

1. Sterilise everything that will come into contact with your wine.
2. Extract juice/flavours from the fruit/flowers.
3. Add sugar, water and possibly additives, such as a Campden Tablet.
4. Add yeast.
5. Start the first fermentation, often in the bucket.
6. Strain, often to a demijohn with an airlock fitted, and leave for the second fermentation which will last from anything from 1-3 months.
7. Strain off the sediment again (sometimes this isn't necessary) and leave to mature for another 2-3 months.
8. Bottle and leave for a further 2-3 months or more.
9. Drink.

There are a number of optional other steps, depending on the recipe. Some people choose to filter their wine before they bottle it. Some use particular additives (which we'll come on to later), some don't. But this, essentially, is the process.

Preparing Hedgerow Fruits

The main difference between working with hedgerow fruits and cultivated fruits from the supermarket is preparing them. Whilst gathering the ingredients can be dreamy on a warm sunny afternoon, small foraged fruits can be fiddly to deal with once you get them home. Compared with (say) chopping apples or strawberries, pressing crab apples whilst trying to avoid breaking the pips can feel a bit faffy. Rest assured, the effort is totally worth it.

Collecting and Preparing Hedgerow Fruits for Winemaking
When collecting fruit, pick in the cleanest places you can. So avoid busy roadsides with traffic fumes. Pick your fruit higher than a dog's leg can reach, if you get my drift. The good news is you can wash fruit quite easily under the tap, unlike flowers. But I still prefer to start with the cleanest fruit I can find.

When you get home, pick through what you have collected. Remove any twigs, leaves or any fruit which has started to go soft, rot or has any signs of mould or insects. Anything you can't use can be composted. Depending on which recipe you are following, some fruits may need to be cut up before use. Others, like soft berries, can be used whole. And at this stage, you could freeze your fruits.

Freezing Fruit
Many people always freeze their fruit before they use it to make wine. When it is frozen, the water in the fruit expands, and the ice crystals puncture and break the cell walls. This can enable more juice to be released. It also means you don't need to crush the fruit very much, if at all, to release the juice.

Another benefit of freezing your fruit is that you can collect it in stages until you have enough to make a batch of wine from it. And if your blackberry picking goes into Sunday evening and you can't make wine until next weekend: no problem. Just freeze the fruit until you are ready to make it.

Extracting Juice from Hedgerow Fruit
Sometimes you need to extract the juice from your fruit to make wine, rather than just adding the whole fruit to the bucket. Freezing can help with this, as explained above. But if you break the seeds, they can make your wine bitter.

So you need to use a gentle extraction method to ensure you don't damage the seeds. The following works very well.

Extracting Juice

These instructions are from a recipe for one standard demijohn (4.5 litres or 6 bottles) of wine. Simply adapt the amount of boiling water you add depending on the recipe you are following.

You will need:
- 1x straining bag, big enough to take your fruit
- 2x food grade buckets.
- A loose fitting lid for one bucket or a clean tea towel
- some pegs to secure your straining bag to the top of the bucket.

Instructions
- Sterilise all the equipment you are about to use.
- Put your fruit in the straining bag and tie the top with string.
- Put the bag inside one fermentation bucket, with the tied bit hanging over the side so it doesn't fall in.
- Secure the bag to the rim of the bucket with pegs.
- Pour over boiling water. I look at how much water the recipe suggests I need, and pour one third of that amount over the fruit.
- Cover the bucket with a loose fitting lid or tea towel and allow to cool.
- Lift the bag out of the bucket and allow the liquid to drip out.
- When it has almost finished dripping, put the bag into bucket number two.
- Pour over more boiling water (I use the another third of the quantity the recipe asks for), cover the bucket again and leave to cool.
- Lift the bag out of the second bucket, allowing the liquid to drip out.
- Compost what is left of the fruit.
- Mix the two cooled buckets of juice together.

You have now have your juice and can continue adding sugar, sugar syrup or whatever the recipe says. If you now need to dissolve sugar in water for your recipe, you have the remaining third in which to do that.

I realise this all sounds a bit fiddly and time consuming. In reality it only takes a few minutes, in fact it takes longer to explain it than it takes to do it. It is waiting for things to cool down that takes the most time.

Wine from Hedgerow Flowers

Before I started actually making wine, it was the idea of making it from flowers that appealed to me the most. Such a romantic notion: taking beautifully fragranced flowers and turning them into wine.

In reality, making wine from flowers can be pretty fiddly and time-consuming. If you imagine just how many Hawthorn (aka May) flowers you need to fill a bucket - a lot - you can imagine the time it takes to pick and prepare them. This will include removing the stems, which have a tendency to make your wine bitter. Making wine from flowers can be a true labour of love but I urge you to try it, with a good tried and tested recipe.

As with hedgerow fruit, pick your flowers in the cleanest areas you can. Fresh flowers should ideally be picked in the morning, in full sun. They need to be used soon after you have picked them, they don't like hanging around. And unlike fruits, which you can freeze as you gather them, many flower petals go black once frozen. The exceptions to this are dandelion petals, which can be frozen in batches and used when you're ready. For some recipes you can substitute dried flowers, but these can be difficult to source. For all these reasons I often make half batches of fresh flower wine in 2.5 litre buckets, so I don't need so many flowers and can get the fermentation going quickly.

However I do make full batches of elderflower wine. I have stood for long periods with a fork removing tiny flowers from their bitter stems, and the wines and champagnes were definitely worth it. Naturally, I've included an elderflower champagne recipe in this journal. Ah, the excitement of elderflower champagne. Lots of people have their first homebrewing experience with this. It is quick, easy and you don't need lots of flowers for it. Family legend has it that my Mum's champagne exploded in the wardrobe. This may explain why I don't recall her making it often.

You can avoid explosions by using PET plastic bottles. They swell to let you know when fizz levels are high, you then 'burp' them by releasing the lids now and again. Storing elderflower champagne in recycled, plastic lemonade bottles won't win design awards, but it is easier and safer than dealing with shards of broken glass around the house where elderflower champagne bottles have exploded. You have been warned!

Foraging

Foraging for ingredients and turning them into something wonderful to drink is a pastime I can thoroughly recommend.

If you have never foraged before, don't panic. The term 'foraging' can mean many things to different people. I'm not talking about becoming a nomad and living off the land as our ancestors did, as attractive as that sounds some days. I'm talking about picking easily-identifiable fruits and flowers to make wine. The countryside is packed with delicious edibles, from elderflowers in Spring to sloes in Autumn. You don't have to be a trained botanist to do this.

You can make wine from all sorts of things, but we are sticking with species which are easy to identify. In fact, I've never really moved on to the trickier stuff when it comes to wine making. My view is: if it tastes nice just picked, it could make nice wine. If it tastes unpleasant when picked, being fermented is unlikely to improve the taste much. The exceptions to this rule are sloes which taste horrid raw, yet make fantastic wine and, of course, sloe gin.

If you are new to this, find yourself some easily identifiable fruits and flowers and stick to those to start with. I have included a basic foraging calendar for winemakers later in this journal - just pick off a couple of those and get going. Bear in mind that these calendars are a general guide. I'm in Southern England. If you're in North West Scotland your berries may come later than mine.

Forage responsibly. Only harvest what you plan to use, leave behind more than you take, avoid disturbing plant roots. Leave plenty for the birds and ensure you adhere to the Code of Conduct for the Conservation and Enjoyment of Wild Plants. Most importantly, never pick any wild plant unless you are 100% certain you have correctly identified it. For the avoidance of doubt, this journal is not intended to help you identify fruits and flowers. You need a good guide (maybe a human one if you're completely new to all this) to do that. You will find book recommendations on our website at AlmostOffGrid.com.

That 'only harvest what you plan to use' statement is important. When you stumble across a tree heaving with beautiful ripe fruits, the temptation will be to pick masses of them. Taking a small set of battery operated kitchen scales on your walks can keep you focused, allowing for any fruit which, once you get it home, may not be quite to standard.

The Winemaker's Foraging Calendar

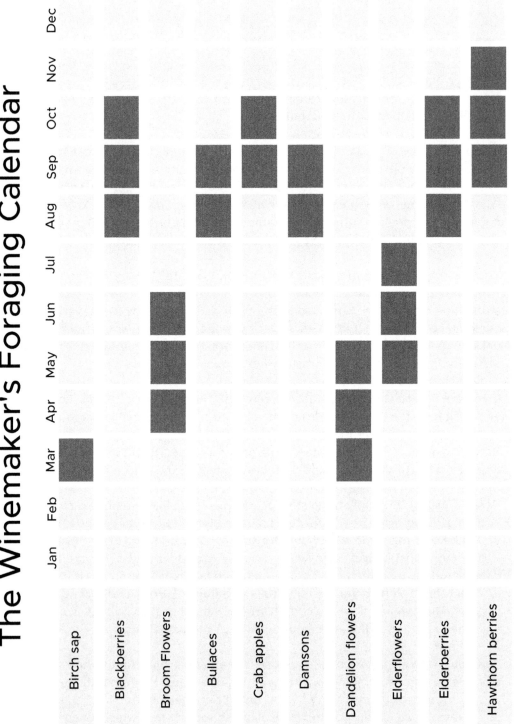

The Winemaker's Foraging Calendar

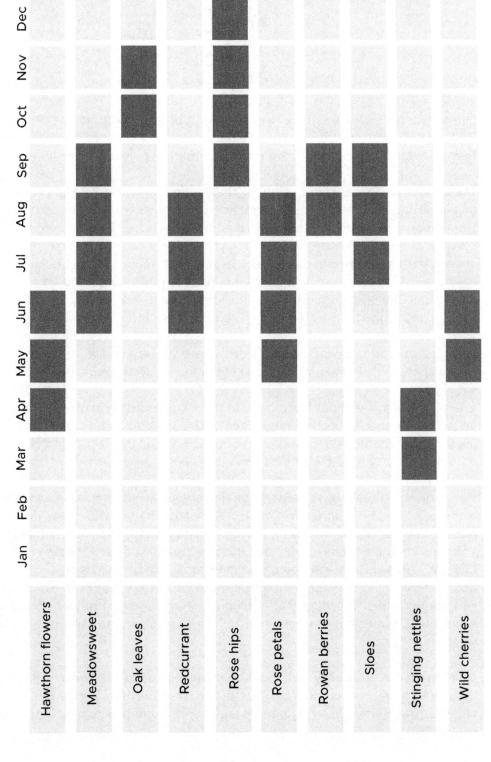

	Jan	Feb	Mar	Apr	May	Jun	Jul	Aug	Sep	Oct	Nov	Dec
Hawthorn flowers				■	■	■	■	■	■			
Meadowsweet						■	■	■	■			
Oak leaves						■				■	■	
Redcurrant						■	■	■				
Rose hips									■	■	■	■
Rose petals					■	■		■				
Rowan berries								■	■			
Sloes							■	■	■			
Stinging nettles			■	■								
Wild cherries					■	■						

Brewing with the Seasons

Every year we stumble upon a new foraging opportunity somewhere on a walk - a wild plum tree, a sloe bush, a patch of meadowsweet. We used to think we would remember where it was the following year. We never did.

These days we make a note of our exact location for future reference. We do this using the what3words app. What3words gives every 3 metre square location on earth a unique three-word address. It is used by many emergency services in the UK to identify a location with a much greater degree of accuracy than using a postal address, or giving directions. Whilst being able to find these damsons again next year might not really constitute an emergency, the app is incredibly useful for foraging. Particularly for fruits, flowers and fungus growing in the same place year after year.

Download the What3words app, record where you are and what you've found, then you'll easily find that exact location in future years. Perfect.

You can read more about foraging with the what3words app on our blog. What3words also works brilliantly when you're walking in the spring and identify, say, the flowers on a blackthorn bush. When you return in the autumn, with any luck it will be a bush covered in sloe berries.

Whilst on the subject of seasons, sometimes you'll want to make a wine with a combination of fruits that are not in season together, or with fruits that are not currently available. A freezer comes into its own for this. Simply freeze your blackberries, for example, until the sloes are in season. Freezing fruit in this way can help to break down the fibres in the fruit, which is an added bonus. It means you will be able to get more juice from your fruit, which is why some recipes specifically advise you to freeze the fruit before you make wine with it. We use a vacuum sealer before freezing so the fruits don't take up loads of space.

Dried fruits can work very well too. So when I'm making a mixed berry wine, the blackberries may come from my freezer, the elderberries might be dried and the strawberries and raspberries may come from the supermarket.

Seasonal Brewing Plan

Spring

Summer

Autumn

Winter

Glossary of Terms

Ageing - storing the wine when it has finished fermenting, either in the fermentation vessel or in bottles, to give it time to mature until it is ready to drink.

Bottle conditioning - the process of carbonating wine in the bottle by adding sugar which creates carbon dioxide (CO_2).

Bottle shock - a temporary condition in which the taste of wine changes after being bottled and/or transported - worth bearing in mind when you are gifting your homemade wine. See our blog for more details.

Bulk ageing - storing the wine to age in a large vessel rather than bottling.When you age your wine in the bucket or demijohn you reduce the amount of time it is exposed to the air, which is why some people prefer it.

Carboy - a food-grade glass or plastic fermentation vessel.

Demijohn - a food-grade glass or plastic fermentation vessel with a narrow neck, in which some people also age their wine once fermentation is finished.

Decant - gradually pour from one vessel to another to separate the wine from sediment which may have formed whilst the wine is aging in the bottle. Decanting red wine can also improve its flavour and aroma by exposing the wine to the air for a period of time.

Degassing - the process of removing carbon dioxide. Carbon dioxide forms naturally in winemaking and can negatively affect the final taste. Degassing is usually done by agitating the liquid to release carbon dioxide. It can be done with a spoon/paddle or a degassing wand.

Fermentation - the process by which yeast feeds on sugar to produce alcohol and carbon dioxide (CO_2).

Final Gravity - measurement of the amount of sugar left in your wine when it has finished fermenting. Also known as Finishing Gravity or FG.

Hydrometer- an instrument that measures the sugar content of your wine, helping you to determine its alcohol content. A hydrometer can also let you know with reasonable certainty when fermentation has finished.

The lees - the left-over solids and yeast which lay as sediment in the bottom of a demijohn or brewing bucket.

The must - the mixture of ingredients you start with (such as sugar, crushed fruit, herbs) which eventually turn into wine.

Oxidation - the change in wine when it is exposed to oxygen. When a bottle is opened and then re-corked, the contents change and can become overly oxidised and this changes the taste.

Pitching - adding the yeast to the must to begin fermentation. Some yeasts need rehydrating with water to create a 'starter'. But most modern yeasts can simply be sprinkled on the surface of the must and stirred in, which makes this a very simple process. The other advantage of adding yeast in this way is that you reduce the potential for contamination.

Priming sugar - sugar added at the bottling stage to carbonate in drinks such as elderflower champagne (recipe on page 40).

Racking - the process of syphoning wine from one vessel to another, or into bottles, leaving the sediment behind.

Starting Gravity or SG - measurement of the amount of sugar in your wine before the yeast starts to consume it, turning it into alcohol. Also known as Opening Gravity/Original Gravity or OG.

Sterilising - also known as sanitising or disinfecting, this is the important process of treating all equipment coming into contact with the wine to ensure it is perfectly clean. More about this on page 21.

Stuck fermentation - when wine begins fermenting normally but then stops before you expect it to, or starts up again when you thought it had finished, or doesn't start at all. Temperature is the most common culprit, but see our blog post https://bit.ly/10ReasonsStopped for more advice on this.

Additives in Wine Making

The recipes in this book are designed for beginners. When you decide to move on from basic recipes, you will soon discover all sorts of additives in the lists of ingredients.

It is no secret that I'm not a great fan of some home brewing additives. For example, I would prefer to leave a homemade wine to clear naturally, for as long as it takes, rather than add finings (a chemical that speeds up the clearing process). There is nothing wrong with adding finings. It is an efficient way to clear your wine. If you leave your wine for months, it may end up just as clear without the finings. It depends how much time you have, and whether you're prepared to take the chance.

Not all chemicals are the enemy in winemaking. Without cleaning and sterilising chemicals, we might end up with unwanted bacteria in our wine which could spoil the whole batch. Without pectin enzyme added early on in the (say) parsnip winemaking process, the wine may simply never clear.

Wines made from grapes that are pleasant to drink usually have a balance of acids and tannins, as winemaking grapes contain those qualities naturally. Perhaps that's why grapes caught on for winemaking in the first place. Wines made from other ingredients can taste out of balance or as though there's something missing, and additives can plug that gap and vastly improve the final taste of your hedgerow wines.

So some additives I use, and some I don't. It is a personal choice. The list in this journal clarifies what these chemicals are designed to do. You can decide whether or not you wish to use them. Or find an alternative, where one exists.

Bear in mind that some additives are designed to stop fermentation completely. If you don't add them, you must leave your wine for longer before bottling to avoid explosions (see wine making FAQs on page 44). Also, sulphites act as a preservative. Your wine made without them may deteriorate quite quickly.

List of Additives

Acid blend is a mixture of citric, malic, and tartaric acid. A recipe may call for one or more of these acids to be added separately.

Bentonite is a clay used for clearing and stabilising wine. It attaches to yeast particles and falls with them to the bottom of the fermenting vessel to form a sediment, helping to clear your wine. Bentonite is suitable for vegetarian and vegan winemaking (see finings later).

Campden tablets are usually made from potassium or sodium metabisulphite, Campden tablets have a number of uses, both in the making of the wine and the sterilising of equipment.

Citric acid is the main acid in fruits such as currants, elderberries, and strawberries as well as citrus fruits. It is added for flavour and also helps to promote fermentation.

Fermentation stopper aka potassium sorbate. Potassium sorbate is a yeast inhibitor that prevents bacteria from dividing and producing new cells. It is designed to stop fermentation before bottling. It is usually recommended that you add Campden tablets as well as a fermentation stopper to maximise the likelihood that your fermentation has stopped. Some manufacturers also advise that, when using potassium sorbate, you should use Campden tablets at the same time to avoid a duranium (metallic) smell in your wine.

Finings gather proteins and sediment and then sink to the bottom, helping wine to clear more quickly. Finings often contain ingredients derived from animals, which is why most commercial wines cannot be labelled as vegetarian/vegan. For example, gelatine is usually derived from animal body parts, isinglass from fish bladders, and albumen is derived from egg whites. Bentonite clay is a vegan option that can be used to clear wine. The alternative to using any finings at all is time. So leaving your wine to clear naturally for as long as it takes, plus you could also choose to filter it. This is why commercial wine producers tend to use finings, because the alternatives take more time.

Malic acid is the main acid in fruits such as apples, rhubarb, and blackberries. It helps with the fermentation and maturing of the wine.

Pectic enzyme occurs naturally in fruit. It helps your jam to set and can create a haze, neither of which you want when wine making. Pectic enzyme decomposes the pectin in fruit or vegetables to help speed up the clearing of your wine later on.

Precipitated chalk aka calcium carbonate is used to reduce the acidity in wines, particularly when using acidic fruits like rhubarb and apples.

Super wine yeast compound is a blend of bentonite, wine yeast, yeast nutrient, vitamins, and minerals, and is designed to speed up fermentation and clearing. If you use super wine yeast compound, you don't need to add yeast separately as it is already included in this blend.

Tannin occurs naturally in fruit skins, more in red than white fruits, and gives the wine its astringency. Red wines need it for depth. Tannin also combines with proteins in the brewing process to help to clear the wine.

Tartaric acid is found in grapes and dried fruits derived from grapes and it adds flavour to wine.

Yeast is the most well-known additive in winemaking. One is the ambient yeast which exists naturally on the fruit. For example, you can make elderflower champagne using yeasts naturally present on the flowers. However the other, cultured yeast, is more widely used in wine making. And when you use it, this typically involves sterilising the fruit juice to kill the natural yeasts, then replacing them with the cultured yeast from a packet.

The main reason for doing this is predictability. Naturally produced yeasts can be volatile. Even if they work well in one batch of wine, it can be virtually impossible to produce the same result twice. Plus if you have undesirable bacteria in your fruit or flowers it could spoil the whole batch. This is probably why cultured yeasts became so popular and widely used. If you follow the same process, the same yeast usually gives a similar/the same result. If you liked a recipe the first time, you can keep recreating it again and again.

Yeast nutrient is often included in homemade wine recipes. It is not yeast, but rather it is food for the yeast. Yeast nutrient feeds yeast from the start, to ensure fermentation starts quickly and a vigorous fermentation is maintained. If you use yeast nutrient, you still need to add yeast separately.

Wine Making Equipment

You don't need much equipment to start making wine. As with most hobbies, you can make this as complicated (or expensive) as you like, but the good news is you need very little equipment to get going. If you have brewed wine, beer or cider before, you may already have most of it.

If you haven't brewed before and are starting from nothing, we sell a variety of kits for beginners at AlmostOffGrid.com.

If you have brewed before but are unsure what you need for wine, this is what we typically include in our kits in different combinations:

A homebrewing demijohn (4.5 litres/1 gallon), ideally two so you can syphon from one to the other later,

or

A food-grade fermentation bucket (5 litre) - again ideally two so you can syphon wine from the first bucket into the second later. Brewing buckets need a tight-fitting lid with a bored hole and grommet so an airlock can be fitted to the bucket.

Or you could start your wine in a bucket, and finish it in a demijohn.

An airlock and bung. If you're using buckets, you won't need the bung.

A syphon, which can be as simple as a piece of food-grade plastic tubing. We recommend a syphon with a tap and sediment trap which will make things quicker, easier and minimise waste.

A funnel that fits into the top of your chosen bottles.

A stirring paddle or spoon with a long handle. This will be sterilised regularly, so plastic is recommended. Wooden spoons look the part but, after repeated sterilising, they start to disintegrate. So plastic is better for this.

A corker is a device enabling you to fit standard corks into bottles safely, without having to soak the corks first. Search "twin handle" or "twin lever".

Corks. When making wine from a kit that only needs a few weeks in the bottle before drinking, reusing screw caps is fine. However, wines made from scratch benefit from maturing in the bottle for a few months at least, especially when using some of the more bitter fruits such as sloes. So we recommend saving wine bottles into which standard corks will fit to avoid leaks or oxidation. A correctly-fitted cork will allow your bottles to sit for as long as they need to. Always ensure fermentation has completely finished before bottling, to avoid explosions.

Bottles. We sell wine bottles, though we try hard not to. Recycled wine bottles are perfectly fine for homemade wine - start saving now! Check that standard corks fit in the top. Bear in mind that screw top bottles are not designed for corks and may shatter when you try to fit a cork, so are best avoided.

Labels. You can create your own designs and print them yourself, or buy labels ready-printed. Whatever you do, label your wine with what is inside the bottle, and the date you made it to avoid finding random bottles later. That way, if it tastes great, you'll know how to recreate it. We don't always bottle our wine, sometimes we bulk age it in the demijohn in which we made it, replacing the airlock and bung with a solid bung once we're sure fermentation has completely stopped. With wine kits, we have been known to pour it in the glass straight from the bucket, but that's another story. A really simple way to label buckets and demijohns is with brown kraft paper tags, tied on with string. I use them for homebrewing because there's lots of space to write and tick off each step of the recipe as I complete it, so I know where I am in the process.

A hydrometer (optional). This is a tool to measure your wine's sugar content, to confirm fermentation has finished. It also allows you to work out the final alcohol content, by taking a reading at the beginning of the process, then again at the end, and doing a calculation with the readings. If you're not worried about knowing the alcohol content of your finished wine and are happy to leave it for a long time to ensure fermentation has finished, then you don't need a hydrometer. But they do come in handy.

Basic utensils. You will also need some basics which you probably already have in your kitchen. Depending on the recipe, you may for example need a large saucepan, a sieve, butter muslin for straining, a lemon squeezer/juicer, a jug, and some sort of large vessel in which you can sterilise your equipment and bottles. My Dad uses the bath. You don't need to get too technical about this.

Be sure to read a recipe fully before you start making your wine, to ensure you have all the equipment you need. It is not ideal to discover halfway through the process that you're missing something important.

Sterilising

When making wine, the usual basic hygiene rules apply as they would for any food and drink preparation. So ensure your hands are washed before you start, and wash again at regular intervals throughout the process.

Fermenting liquids are an ideal breeding ground for bacteria. Unwanted bacteria will spoil your wine. It will spoil one bottle if the bottle isn't clean, or the lot if the bucket isn't clean. So whatever you are making, you must sterilise everything that comes into contact with your wine. That includes buckets, mixing paddles, bottles, corks, everything.

There are a variety of cleaner/sterilisers to choose from, all of which are simple to use and tend to work in a similar way. If you've ordered a Starter Kit from us, a cleaner/steriliser will be included. Simply follow the instructions on the tub.

If you've never done it before, sterilising sounds like a lot of work. In reality it's easy, and you quickly become used to doing it every time you make something.

I'd advise you to sterilise as you go along. So to begin with you will sterilise the equipment you need to start your wine fermenting, but you won't sterilise the bottles until the wine is ready to bottle. We use the bucket in which we plan to ferment to sterilise the airlock, spoon and so on at the beginning of the process so they are all ready together

Regardless of whether the instructions say to rinse off the sterilising liquid, we always rinse everything thoroughly in cold water after sterilising and just before use.

When making wine you often need to stir the must at different stages. Each time, your spoon must be sterile. There are a couple of ways you can do this. One is to boil a kettle and pour it over the spoon before you use it, as boiling water kills most things. Another way is to keep cleaner/steriliser in a spray bottle and spray the spoon when you need it.

Hedgerow Wine Making Tips

<u>Airlocks should be about half-filled with water</u> to prevent air and fruit flies from entering the bucket or demijohn. The exact level is not critical.

<u>Airlocks caps</u>, which are usually red, stop dust from entering the airlock. They are not designed to be airtight.

<u>The chlorine in tap water can kill yeast</u> so we use bottled, filtered, spring, or previously boiled water that has been allowed to cool. Many will tell you they use tap water. It depends on your water supply.

<u>You know fermentation has begun</u> when the air starts pushing up through the airlock and you hear a bubbling or 'bloop' sound.

<u>Knowing fermentation has finished</u> can be more difficult to judge. The airlock will usually stop blooping after 2-3 months. Sometimes sooner, sometimes later. To be certain it has finished, you can add fermentation stopper and a Campden tablet before bottling your wine. Another way to know is to take a hydrometer reading. If the reading is the same for 3 days running, that suggests fermentation has finished. And the final way, which is the way we use, is to leave the wine until there has been no sign of life in the vessel and airlock for ages. Whichever method you use to be sure fermentation has finished, be certain it has before you bottle to avoid the dreaded exploding bottles. See more about this in Wine Making FAQs on page 44.

<u>Maintain the fermentation</u> by storing the vessel in a warm-ish place if it is cold. Otherwise standard room temperature is fine, out of sunlight. Customers often contact us in the winter to say they're having problems starting/maintaining, fermentation. The problem in winter is, more often than not, temperature.

<u>The purpose of racking</u> is to move the wine into another sterile vessel, leaving the sediment behind. A homebrewing syphon with sediment trap and tap is not only easier than a simple tube, but it also avoids wasting wine (hooray!).

<u>When sealing the bottles</u> standard corks are best for wine making. Sterilise them briefly before use. Don't soak them, as they may start to disintegrate.

Consider investing in nylon straining bags which are strong, easy to sterilise and re-usable. They simplify removing fruit and flowers from the bucket, and stop pips and stones getting in to your wine only to turn up in unwanted places later. Simply compost the contents of the bag, then wash and re-use it.

Maintain the fermentation by storing the vessel in a warm-ish place if it is cold outside. Otherwise standard room temperature is fine, out of sunlight.

Leave 24 hours between using Campden tablets and adding yeast. Many recipes will say to add a crushed Campden tablet to the mix before adding yeast, and to leave 24 hours in-between. Campden tablets kill unwanted bacteria and yeasts. After 24 hours the Campden will have dissipated, then you can add yeast. Any sooner and you risk killing it.

Reuse bottles that previously had corks fitted for winemaking. Now if you've bought a wine kit from me and I've told you that old screw topped bottles and caps are fine, it may sound like I'm contradicting myself. But the key is not to attempt to use corks with screw top bottles. We have heard horror stories of people forcing a cork into a bottle designed for a screw cap, and the bottle shattering. Screw capped bottles are not designed for corks. We don't advocate using screw caps for hedgerow wines because you will need to lay this wine down for a good few months, possibly years. A re-used screw cap can allow air in and/or leak over time, which is why corks are what you need.

Leave your wine to mature for at least 3 months before tasting. Fruit wines with a heavy natural tannin content, like damsons, will need at least a year before they taste any good. I know. But it is worth the wait. The longer you leave it, the better it will be. If you really can't bear to wait and open your wines sooner than this, do yourself a favour and keep a bottle back. Hide it from yourself for a year or more, then try it. You'll be amazed at the difference.

Time solves most problems. If you taste your wine at the point of bottling and are not wildly impressed, keep the faith, carry on and leave it to mature for as long as possible. You gain nothing by chucking it down the sink now, and the chances are you'll be pleasantly surprised later on. Damson wine was like that for us. After 1 year: meh. After 2.5 years: amazing.

Blackberry Claret Recipe

Makes
4.5 Litres/6 bottles

Ingredients

- 1.5lb (0.75kg) blackberries
- 250ml bottle red grape juice concentrate
- 3/4lb/0.5kg granulated sugar
- 1 teaspoon pectic enzyme
- 1 teaspoon red wine yeast (or any dried active or all-purpose wine yeast)
- bottled/spring/filtered/boiled water to 4.5 litres
- 1 Campden tablet and/or fermentation stopper (optional)

Equipment

- a 5 litre food grade bucket with bored lid and grommet
- a second food grade bucket to prepare the fruit
- a standard 4.5 litre demijohn (with bored cap if you're using a PET demijohn)
- an airlock (and bored bung if you're using a glass demijohn)
- cleaner/steriliser
- a straining bag and funnel
- a pan, a stirring spoon, plus a bottle for any left-over juice
- a syphon
- bottles
- labels

Method

1. Sterilise all equipment that will come into contact with the wine.
2. To extract the juice from your blackberries: put them in a straining bag and tie the top with string.
3. Put the tied bag into one of the buckets with the tied end hanging over the edge.
4. Pour 2 litres of boiling water over the blackberry bag and leave to cool.
5. Once cool enough to handle, lift the bag and allow the juice to drain. Then move the bag into the second bucket.
6. Pour 1.5 litres of boiling water over the bag, leave to cool.
7. Meanwhile, boil another half litre of water in a saucepan and add the sugar. Stir until the sugar has dissolved.
8. Leave all three vessels to cool. When all at room temperature (buckets 1 & 2 plus saucepan with sugar), squeeze the bag of berries gently into bucket 2 to extract the last juice. Compost the de-juiced blackberries. This all sounds a bit faffy. In reality it only takes a few minutes, cooling takes the longest time.
9. Pour the cool sugar water into the demijohn, using the funnel.
10. Add the two buckets of juice, leaving a 3 inch gap at the top.
11. Put any remaining blackberry juice into the sterilised extra bottle for left-over juice. Seal and keep it in the fridge in case you need to top up.
12. Add the pectin enzyme and yeast to the demijohn, give it a swirl and fit the bung and airlock with water in it.
13. Leave in a warmish place and fermentation will start.
14. When fermentation has slowed down after 3 days or so, top up the demijohn to shoulder height with the extra juice.
15. Replace the airlock and place the demijohn out of sunlight and at room temperature. Leave to ferment out and clear for at least 3 months.
16. When you are confident fermentation has stopped and the wine is clear, prepare to bottle. Optional: add a crushed Campden tablet and fermentation stopper to be certain.
17. Rack the wine into sterilised bottles, leaving the sediment behind.
18. Seal the bottles with standard corks and label.
19. Leave the wine to mature for at least 9 months. The longer you can leave it, the better it will taste.

Blackberry Claret Notes

27

Damson Wine

Makes
4.5 Litres/6 bottles

Ingredients

- 1.5kg damsons, destemmed, destoned and frozen
- 0.5kg sultanas, left whole
- 1.25kg sugar
- Up to 3 litres of water
- One half teaspoon acid blend
- One teaspoon yeast nutrient
- One teaspoon pectic enzyme
- 1 campden tablet
- Half a sachet of red wine yeast
- 6 teaspoons glycerol

Equipment

- 1 straining bag
- 1 x 5 litre food grade bucket
- 1 x demijohn
- an airlock and bung
- cleaner/steriliser
- a saucepan
- a stirring spoon and a potato masher
- a syphon
- bottles
- labels

Method

1. Sterilise all equipment to come into contact with the wine.
2. Put the frozen damsons in the straining bag.
3. Put the bag in the bucket to defrost, to capture all the juice as the berries melt.
4. Once defrosted, mash with a sterilised potato masher to release more juice.
5. Heat 2 litres of the water with the sugar in a saucepan, stirring with the spoon until the sugar has dissolved.
6. Pour the hot sugarwater over the damsons in the bag, in the bucket. Stir and leave to cool to room temperature.
7. Add the campden tablet, stir and leave for 12 hours with a clean tea towel over the top to keep dust and fruit flies out.
8. Add the sultanas, acid blend, yeast nutrient and pectic enzyme, put the tea towel over and leave for another 12 hours.
9. Sprinkle the yeast on the must, put the tea towel back on again and leave for a further 7 days, stirring daily.
10. After 7 days, lift the bag out and allow the liquid to drain back into the bucket. You can compost the damsons and sultanas.
11. Transfer the wine to the sterilised demijohn. If it doesn't reach the shoulders of the demijohn, top up with a little water.
12. Fit a sterilised bung plus airlock with water in it.
13. Leave to ferment for at least a month.
14. If there seems to be a lot of sediment in the bottom, which there often is with damsons, rack the wine after a month or so leaving the sediment behind and refit the lid and airlock.
15. Leave for 2-3 months more, racking again if sediment builds.
16. When you are confident fermentation has stopped and the wine has cleared, prepare to bottle. Optional: add a crushed Campden tablet and fermentation stopper to be certain.
17. Bottle your wine, adding one teaspoon of glycerol per bottle. This will improve the mouthfeel of this wine enormously.
18. Label and leave to mature for at least a year. The longer you can leave it, the better it will be!

Note about Damson wine: this was one of the first we made. After a year it was 'meh' and I almost poured it down the sink. After 2 years it was delicious. Keep the faith on this one!

Damson Wine Notes

Dandelion Wine

Makes
4.5 Litres/6 bottles

Ingredients

- a one gallon container full of freshly picked dandelion flowers
- 3 lemons (zest and juice)
- 1 orange (zest and juice)
- 200ml white grape juice concentrate
- 1.5kg sugar - standard white granulated is fine
- 1 sachet of white wine yeast
- yeast nutrient
- bottled/spring/filtered/boiled water to 4.5 litres
- 1 Campden tablet and/or fermentation stopper (optional)

Equipment

- 1x 5 litre food grade bucket
- bored lid that fits the bucket, with grommet fitted in hole
- an airlock
- a demijohn with bored bung
- cleaner/steriliser
- a large pan
- a stirring spoon
- butter muslin and a sieve
- a funnel
- a syphon
- bottles
- labels

Method

1. Remove the petals from the dandelion heads. If remove them from each flower in one go, it won't take as long as you think!
2. Sterilise all equipment that will be used.
3. Pour 1 litre of boiling water into a bucket, add the dandelion petals. Cover loosely and leave for 24 hours, stirring occasionally.
4. Boil 2.5 litres of water in a pan, add the sugar, stir until dissolved, allow to cool.
5. Add the sugar water to the dandelion water in the bucket, together with the lemon and orange juice, zest and grape juice concentrate.
6. Add the yeast and yeast nutrient according to the packet instructions.
7. Cover loosely again and leave for another 2-3 days, stirring occasionally.
8. Using the sieve, funnel and muslin, strain the wine into the demijohn.
9. Check the level. Top up to the shoulders of the demijohn with water if needed.
10. Fit the bung to the demijohn, then add water to the airlock and fit it to the bung.
11. Leave the demijohn in a reasonably warm place. You will know fermentation has started when the airlock starts to bubble.
12. Place the fermenting wine in a spot out of sunlight at room temperature, and leave it to ferment out for 2 months.
13. Sterilise the first bucket again and syphon the wine into it, leaving the sediment behind (known as racking off). You can either clean and sterilise the original demijohn again and put the racked wine back in it, or leave it in the bucket. Either way, if the water level is low without the sediment then top up again with water.
14. Refit the bung/lid and airlock and leave for a further 2 months to clear.
15. When you are confident fermentation has stopped and the wine is clear, prepare to bottle. Optional: add a crushed Campden tablet and fermentation stopper to be sure.
16. Bottle your wine and label.
17. Leave for a couple of weeks to recover from bottling. This wine is best drunk young.

Dandelion Wine Notes

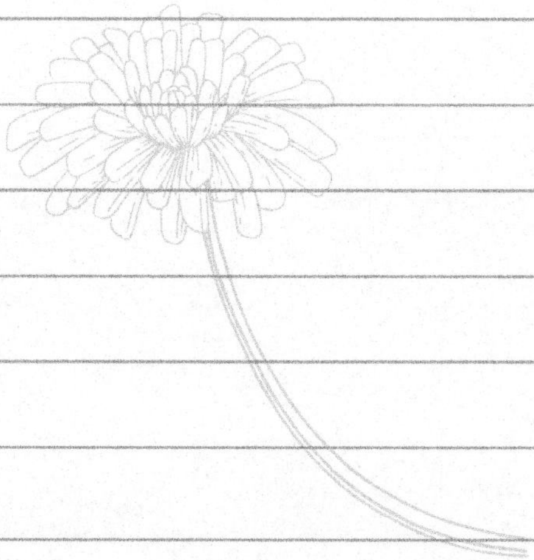

Elderberry Wine

Makes
4.5 Litres/6 bottles

Ingredients

- 1kg elderberries
- 1.25kg sugar
- 1 lemon
- 1 Campden tablet
- pectic enzyme
- yeast nutrient
- 1 sachet of red wine yeast
- bottled/spring/filtered/boiled water to 4.5 litres
- A second Campden tablet and/or fermentation stopper (optional)

Equipment

- 1 x 5 litre food grade bucket
- a bored lid that fits the bucket, plus grommet
- 1 demijohn
- 1 bored bung
- an airlock
- cleaner/steriliser
- a large pan
- a stirring spoon
- a sieve
- butter muslin
- a syphon
- bottles
- labels

Method

1. Freeze the berries overnight, on the stems.
2. Sterilise all equipment that you will use.
3. Take the berries from the freezer and remove them from their stems, rejecting any that are green, squished or mouldy.
4. Put the berries in the bucket, and cover with 2.5 litres of boiling water.
5. Loosely cover the bucket with the lid and leave for 24 hours.
6. Press the berries in the bucket (with your hands or you could use a potato masher), being careful not to crush the seeds.
7. Boil 1.5 litres of water in a pan, add the sugar and stir until dissolved.
8. Add the hot sugar water to the bucket, leave to cool.
9. Strain the mixture through a sieve lined with butter muslin into the demijohn, using the funnel. Leave it for a while to drip through, rather than squeezing the fruit.
10. Add the lemon juice, pectic enzyme and 1 crushed Campden tablet. Fit the bung and airlock, leave for 24 hours.
11. Add the yeast and yeast nutrient to the demijohn. Refit the bung and airlock (with water added to the airlock) and leave in a warm place to ferment for 3-5 days, until the vigorous first fermentation starts to slow down.
12. Check the liquid level in the demijohn, top up with cold boiled/bottled water to shoulder height.
13. Place the demijohn on a surface out of sunlight, at room temperature.
14. Leave the wine to ferment out for around 3 months.
15. Syphon off (rack) the wine back into the resterilised bucket, leaving the sediment behind.
16. You can either refit the lid and airlock to the bucket, or resterilise the demijohn before pouring the wine back into the demijohn and refitting the bung and airlock. Either way, leave for another 2 months to finish fermenting and clear.
17. When you are confident fermentation has stopped and the wine is clear, prepare to bottle. Optional: add a crushed Campden tablet and fermentation stopper to be sure.
18. Syphon off (rack) the wine into sterilised bottles, leaving the sediment behind.
19. Seal the bottles with standard corks and label.
20. Leave the wine to mature for at least 9 months. The longer you can leave it, the better it will taste.

Elderberry Wine Notes

Elderflower Champagne

Makes

10 litres

Ingredients

- 6-8 large elderflower heads (flowers fully opened)
- 1kg /2.2lb sugar
- 2 lemons
- 1 orange
- 5 tablespoons white wine vinegar
- 10 litres cold bottled/filtered/boiled water
- 1 sachet sparkling wine yeast (we use Lalvin EC-1118)

Equipment

- 1 x 25 litre food grade bucket
- a bored lid that fits the bucket plus grommet
- an airlock
- cleaner/steriliser
- a straining bag
- a large pan
- a stirring spoon
- a sieve
- a syphon
- 10x 1 litre or 20x 500ml plastic/PET Bottles with screw caps*
- labels

*Elderflower champagne is notorious for explosions. So PET bottles and screw caps are recommended, rather than glass.

Method

1. Sterilise all equipment that will be used.
2. Separate the flowers from the stems with a fork, removing as much green as possible (the green stems add bitterness).
3. Wash the oranges and lemons, remove the zest and juice them.
4. Warm the water.
5. Put the 10 litres of warm water into the fermentation bucket.
6. Stir in the sugar until dissolved.
7. Add the vinegar, fruit juice and zest.
8. Add the elderflowers to the bucket. Work as gently as you can to avoid crushing the flowers.
9. Sprinkle the wine yeast over the surface of the flower liquid.
10. Gently stir then fit the bucket lid, ensuring it is sealed. Add water to the airlock and fit it into the lid.
11. Leave in a reasonably warm place until fermentation begins.
12. Leave to stand for approx 5-7 days, or until the majority of the bubbling and fizzing has stopped. Check the contents of the bucket daily, stirring any flowers floating on the top back into the liquid with a sterilised spoon and quickly replacing the lid.
13. Place the bucket on a surface higher than the bottles. Use the syphon to move the elderflower champagne into the bottles, leaving an approximate 1.5 inch/3.8cm gap at the top of each bottle. Take care not to disturb the sediment in the bucket and try to avoid transferring any debris*. The less sediment you pick up, the clearer the end result will be.
14. Bottle the champagne into the sterilised PET/plastic bottles, screw on the caps and label.
15. Leave the bottles for 2-3 weeks in a cool place to carbonate.
16. Check for fizz. You can do this by gently unscrewing one cap and listening for the sound of air escaping, which means it's going fizzy. If no fizz, leave for another week. If nothing still, add a half teaspoon of sugar to each bottle, reseal and leave for another 2-3 weeks to carbonate.**
17. Serve cold, with added honey and/or elderflower cordial to 'back-sweeten', if liked.

*if you suspect sediment has made its way into your bottles, store them upright so that, when you open a bottle, the sediment will be inclined to remain at the bottom when you pour.

**don't be tempted to add sugar to the bottles unless you are certain that carbonation isn't happening. Too much fizz will send most of your champagne up the wall rather than into the glass.

Elderflower Champagne Notes

Wine Making FAQs

Hopefully, most of the questions you were asking yourself have been answered. However, I have included some of the questions we get asked in the shop, which haven't been covered elsewhere in this journal.

<u>Should I be concerned about exploding bottles?</u> You may have heard about the exploding elderflower wine in my Mum's wardrobe in about 1973. Usually, this happens because the yeast did not finish its job completely. Then after bottling, the yeast starts up again resulting in an explosion. So you must ensure fermentation has finished before you bottle into glass. This is why we recommend bottling a sparkling wine, such as elderflower champagne, in plastic/PET bottles with screw caps instead. The bottles will tell you if fermentation has restarted because the plastic will become hard and tight as pressure builds. Then you simply release the gas through the screw cap - known as 'burping the bottles'.

<u>Is all this sediment at the bottom of the bucket normal?</u> Yes, totally normal. Sediment is a mixture of dead yeast, additives (if you added them) and fruit bits which have fallen to the bottom. It is not a good idea to leave your wine on sediment for months, as it can affect the taste. So if you plan to age your wine in the bucket or demijohn, rack it off the sediment first. You can then put your sediment on the compost heap.

<u>Do I really need to sterilise everything all the time?</u> Yes. It's the one thing you really must do. Bad bacteria will spoil your wine.

<u>Do I have to leave the wine to mature? Can I drink it sooner?</u> Yes you can, but it won't taste as nice as it could. In a world of instant gratification, hedgerow wines take longer to mature than most wines. But time passes so quickly, it really will be ready to drink before you know it.

<u>Can I use bread yeast in winemaking?</u> You could, but it doesn't work as well as wine yeast. If you literally have nothing else and don't want to buy wine yeast, you can give it a try. But this is one of those "just because you can do it, it doesn't mean you should" situations. We haven't tried it, but we're told bread yeast gives the wine a bready yeasty taste which overwhelms everything else.

Can I add too much yeast to a batch of wine? I don't always specify how much yeast to use in each recipe, as it can depend on the yeast. I typically add about a teaspoon of yeast per 5 litre bucket/4.5 litre demijohn. If you want to be precise, check the yeast packet where it tells you how much the sachet will treat, then calculate how much you need for your batch. If you add lots of yeast, it will only consume the sugar in the vessel, then die and fall to the bottom. An awful lot might affect the taste of the final wine. At worst, the yeast may start up again later resulting in exploding bottles (see earlier FAQ).

How can I create a red wine with more body? When you start making your own recipes at home, you realise you have become used to commercially produced drinks that often contain flavourings and/or additives, particularly those labelled as country or fruit wines. If you're missing the 'body' in a shop-bought wine, look out for recipes with added grape juice concentrate which can really help. Some recipes, like the damson one in this journal, also include adding some glycerol at the bottling stage which, again, really helps with body and mouthfeel.

My wine doesn't taste great. What can I do? Give it more time. Time is your friend in winemaking. It's amazing what another six months can do for a bottle that didn't taste great when you first made it. This is particularly true of wine made with fruits with a high tannin content, such as damsons and elderberries. I talked earlier about the damson wine we made which tasted amazing after a few years. Yes I know you don't want to wait a few years, so start with a wine which takes less time to mature, or a kit wine, whilst you wait for your damson wine to mature. It really will be worth the wait.

What should my wine's Final Gravity be? This will depend on whether you are making a dry, medium or sweet wine. If you are not using a hydrometer, this isn't something you need to worry about. However, if you are using one and you're looking for a rough guide:
- a wine's starting gravity should usually be between 1.070 to 1.090 and the usual finished ABV (alcohol by volume) will be between 10.5% to 13%.
- a wine's finishing gravity would typically be from 0.990 (for dry wines) to 1.005 (for sweet wines).

What if my wine still tastes horrible, even after I've left it for ages? If it's just not to your taste (as opposed to contaminated or 'off'), pour it into a sterile demijohn. Find a bottle of organic vinegar with flaky mother sediment in the bottom. Add that, then put muslin over the neck secured with a rubber band to keep dust out. Leave for 6 months at least. Et voila! Homemade wine vinegar, with a new mother in the bottom which you can use to make another batch of vinegar. So even if you don't like how your wine tastes, nothing is wasted.

Useful Information (and free stuff!)

Visit our Almost Off Grid online shop for all your wine, mead, cider and beer making needs. We sell a variety of kits, yeasts and equipment. Standard, Express, and local delivery options as well as click and collect are all available at:

www.AlmostOffGrid.com

As a thank you for reading this book, a £5 gift voucher will be yours when you sign up to our mailing list at this address:

https://www.almostoffgrid.com/pages/5-off

You can also download free printable labels from our website. You'll find a variety of label designs for your homemade mead, wine, cider and liqueurs here:

https://www.almostoffgrid.com/pages/labels

Visit our blog for more articles and advice on wine making AlmostOffGrid.com including:

- Beginner's Guide to making wine from fruit and flowers
- Elderflower wine recipe
- Blackberry port recipe
- How to rack wine, and why you should
- 10 reasons your fermentation won't start
- 10 reasons why your fermentation may have started and then stopped
- A variety of mead recipes, mead being wine made with honey rather than sugar.

We hope to serve you soon.

Happy Brewing!

73

Printed in Great Britain
by Amazon

84904171R00086